Postal Service Legislative Proposals

American Enterprise Institute for Public Policy Research
Washington, D.C.

ISBN 0-8447-0195-5
Legislative Analysis No. 13, 95th Congress
6 October 1977

Price $2.00 per copy

CONTENTS

INTRODUCTION

Drawing on the tradition of postal monopoly in England, the Continental Congress created our first postal service in 1782.[1] In 1789 the U.S. Constitution gave Congress the power "To establish Post Offices."[2] There followed an enormous expansion of postal service, expansion even beyond apparent need.[3] Yet, throughout the early part of the nineteenth century, the Post Office remained self-supporting and the principle of having total revenues cover total costs became well established.

In the nineteenth century, high postal rates in dense eastern cities were used to subsidize much more costly service in developing southern and western areas. Alternative private express services began to threaten this policy of cross subsidization and perhaps even the survival of the Post Office itself. The Postal Act of 1845 was passed to outlaw such private express service.[4] This was the last important general postal legislation until the Postal Reorganization Act of 1970.[5]

By the middle of the twentieth century the Post Office had come to serve many political purposes, from the employment of war veterans to the subsidization of air travel. Cross subsidization of some classes of mail by other classes, especially by first-class mail, was commonplace. The Post Office Department used old-fashioned mail-handling methods. The quality of its service was widely criticized, and mail service broke down completely for a short time in Chicago in 1966. The large deficits accumulated by the Post Office Department led to a financial crisis.

Under the Postal Reorganization Act of 1970, postal service was removed from politics and placed in the hands of a public corporation, the U.S. Postal Service, to be managed by modern methods. Rates and fees were to be set so that each mail service (except for some public services) would be self-supporting. However, the postal crisis continued after this reorganization, though the deficit anticipated for the most recent year will be but a third of the deficit for the previous year.

Bills now pending before Congress would undo or modify the Postal Reorganization Act of 1970. Some bills would abolish the U.S. Postal Service altogether and reconstitute the Post Office Department as it operated before 1970. Other bills would revamp the current Postal Service and its procedures in various ways.

The two most important bills, H.R. 7700 and S. 1692, would retain the Postal Service but would eliminate the Board of Governors which now oversees Postal Service policy. The board's functions would be divided in different ways among the postmaster general, Congress, and the Postal Rate Commission by the two bills. The two bills would also control the frequency of mail deliveries and have Congress review large capital investments of the Postal Service. They would change rate-making principles and procedures, either to return more control to Congress or to give more discretion to the Postal Rate Commission.

BACKGROUND

Postal Reorganization Act

When postal deficits grew to alarming proportions through the 1960s, President Johnson appointed a Commission on Postal Organization (the Kappel Commission) to study the organization of postal operations. Influenced largely by proposals in the resulting Report of the President's Commission on Postal Organization,[6] Congress sought to remedy this growing problem by removing postal operations from political control and creating a public corporation to provide mail service.

Under provisions of the Postal Reorganization Act of 1970, a Board of Governors appointed by the President, with the consent of the Senate, would choose the postmaster general and oversee operations of the new public enterprise, the United States Postal Service. An independent, expert Postal Rate Commission with members appointed by the President would recommend to the board decisions regarding postal rates and fees and the classification of mail services.

Guidelines were set out in the act that required revenues from each class of mail (except for a few public service categories) to cover the costs that could be attributed or reasonably assigned to that mail class. Since mailers of periodicals had been subsidized, large increases could be expected in their mail rates under the act. A "phasing" period of five years was provided for commercial publications and ten years for publications of nonprofit organizations (later extended to eight and sixteen years), during which time the subsidy for those rates would gradually be withdrawn.[7] For fiscal 1977, $792 million was appropriated for this "phasing" purpose.[8] A $920 million annual appropriation was authorized, essentially to maintain post offices in small communities that would not be self-supporting.[9]

Given these principal provisions of the Postal Reorganization Act, efficient management was thought to be possible. The discretion of postal management was broadened to encourage efficient management. Revenues would be available directly for use by the Postal Service without appropriation. The service was given authority to issue up to $2 billion a year in bonds, $500 million of which could go to pay operating costs. Postal management could undertake capital investments and changes in methods, as long as it provided "prompt, reliable, and efficient services to patrons in all areas."[10] Employees were no longer part of the civil service. They were to be hired and paid according to competence, presumably as in the private sector, and were allowed to bargain collectively with the Postal Service.

Experience under the Act

The years since the birth of the U.S. Postal Service in 1970 have not been easy ones. Unusual increases in the price of fuel and in the general rate of inflation have raised the cost of most products and services. Inflation is said to be perhaps the principal reason for the enormous postal deficits.[11] The wages of the Postal Service's 656,000 employees are indexed to protect them from loss of real income due to inflation. On the other hand, the public service appropriation established with the creation of the Postal Service was a flat amount, with no allowance for inflation. Cost-of-living increases for workers totalled $987,000,000 in just two years.[12] Every one-cent increase in the cost of a gallon of gasoline is said to raise costs by $3,500,000.[13] On the other hand, postal officials feel that steps such as airline deregulation could help reduce postal costs.

When the Postal Service attempted to adjust postal rates in response to these increased costs, the Postal Rate Commission was very slow in processing its requests. The first rate case required seventeen months, and the second took twenty-three months. The Postal Service claims it lost over $1 billion in revenues because of delays in the second proceedings alone.[14] The slow handling of these rate-increase cases may have been due in part to weaknesses in the Postal Service's presentations, but no matter what the causes, the long delays were clearly harmful to sound postal operations.

The Kappel Commission estimated the Postal Service would handle over 100 billion pieces of mail by 1975. Only 91 billion pieces of mail were delivered that year.[15] Decline or lack of growth in mail volume at the same time postal costs were increasing put the Postal Service in a squeeze. Regardless of mail volume, costs climb because of increases in the number of delivery points which must be served.[16] Postal authorities feel savings can be effected by handling mail on an area rather than a local basis.

A major reason the Postal Service has not had enough volume to make for profitable operations has been strong new competition from the development of alternative means of communication.[17] As a participant in the communications market, the Postal Service has been losing business to the telephone since World War II.[18] Total mail volume has not grown appreciably for several years.

The effect of increased volume on profitability is demonstrated by the Postal Service report that its deficit for the fiscal year ending September 30, 1977, will be only $400 million—one-third of the loss for the previous year—because of an increase in mail volume from 89.6 billion pieces to 91.7 billion pieces.[19] The Postal Service faces a host of competitive new technologies, which may achieve dramatic reductions in costs to the users and weaken the monopoly position of the Postal Service.[20] Postal officials, however, do not seem to feel that competing technologies will make great inroads in the near future.

The two main goals of the Postal Reorganization Act were (1) efficient management, and (2) rates for mail service that cover costs; neither seems to have been achieved thus far by the steps that were taken to remove the Postal Service from politics. It is claimed by some that the corporate management of the Postal Service has fared little better than Congress in tying increases in pay to greater productivity and increased efficiency.[21]

The General Accounting Office reported that "overall the mail is moving well, although not as well as in 1969."[22] The Postal Service has turned more to the use of capital equipment to increase productivity and reduce dependence on hand labor. However, labor costs are said to account for nearly 86 percent of total costs.[23] Postal authorities feel that handling more mail on an area basis rather than locally will help reduce the ratio of labor costs. Total employment is being reduced by attrition. Wages were judged by the General Accounting Office to be on a par with those in private industry.

Construction of the National Bulk Mail System at a cost of about $1 billion to speed the handling of parcel post was plagued by cost overruns and by mechanical difficulties.[24] It has not yielded the savings of $300 million per year which had been anticipated.[25] Postal Service officials are concerned that the service's share of parcel deliveries has dropped from about 56 percent of the total to 24 percent. However, its principal competition for the delivery of parcels is now raising its rates, which may help the Postal Service.

Regarding the goal of having postal rates cover costs, the Postal Service has almost seemed determined to avoid compliance with the Postal Reorganization Act and to continue instead with the cross-subsidization practices common before 1970. Cross subsidization among classes of mail was found in Postal Service prices by the Postal Rate Commission's chief administrative law judge in 1975.[26] Avoiding cross subsidization requires sound cost allocation, and the basis for allocating costs to classes of mail used by the Postal Service was ruled unsound and unlawful in the U.S. Court of Appeals for the District of Columbia Circuit in December 1976.[27] This means that, in the six years since it was created, the Postal Service has failed to develop the means of attributing costs to the various classes of mail required by the Postal Reorganization Act.

Two court of appeals decisions after the first two rate cases provide a careful review of the rate-making guidelines in the Postal Reorganization Act and the rate-making practices of the Postal Service and the Postal Rate Commission.[28] Both decisions held that Postal Service practices did not comply with the law. The more recent decision included the following:

> We are an appellate court, not an agency possessed of developed expertise. We look to the design of the Commission's approach not to substitute our judgment for that of the agency, but only to determine whether

> the Commission's adopted method falls unconscionably short of the statutory requirements. . . .
>
> We conclude that in the circumstances of this case the Commission's almost exclusive reliance on a cost variability approach to attribution contravenes a primary purpose of subsection 3622 (b) (3) and therefore fails to comply with the Act. . . .
>
> We conclude that the Commission's present method for assigning unattributable costs proceeds from a faulty premise in contravention of the Act and therefore must be rejected.[29]

Sound costing and pricing is crucially important to the achievement of Postal Reorganization Act goals. With cross subsidization, services priced below their costs (such as publishers' mailings within their home counties and mailings of nonprofit organizations) are such bargains they are demanded in greater quantities, and every unit of such service adds to the postal deficit.[30]

In addition, management incentives are harder to design when rates are not related to costs because the postal revenues of an individual post office do not bear even a crude relationship to the costs incurred there.

The postal deficit rose from $175 million in 1972 to $1,176 million in 1976.[31] It seemed likely to increase despite the closing of small post offices, the reduction of business deliveries in ten East Coast cities, a limitation on overtime work, and other service cuts. With an accumulated deficit at the end of fiscal 1977 looming so large it would exceed assets, Congress acted to relieve another postal crisis by passing the Postal Reorganization Act Amendments of 1976.[32]

1976 Amendments

The Postal Reorganization Act Amendments of 1976 had four main objectives: (1) to relieve the financial crisis of the Postal Service, (2) to improve the Postal Service's reporting to Congress, (3) to modify the Postal Rate Commission and speed its handling of rate requests, and (4) to establish a special Commission on Postal Service to study postal problems.

Relieving the Financial Crisis. The 1976 amendments authorized two appropriations of $500 million each, one to go toward retiring the Postal Service's accumulated operating deficit as of September 30, 1976, and the other for the same purpose for fiscal year 1977. A limitation also was imposed to ensure that the funds would not be used to lower parcel post rates by more than 10 percent below what they would be without the appropriations.

Improving Reporting. In requesting appropriations in the future, the Postal Service is to present to the Committees on Post Office and Civil Service and the Committees on Appropriations of the Senate and the House copies of its budget for the year and a comprehensive statement saying what the Postal Service is doing to comply with its charge to "provide prompt, reliable, and efficient services to patrons in all areas and. . .render postal services to all communities," giving detailed information on operational performance and providing estimates of revenue requirements.

The Postal Service is to appear before the Committees on Post Office and Civil Service of the House and Senate before March 15 of each year to respond to questions relating to its budget and comprehensive statement. The conference committee summed up the reporting need as follows:

> The managers are particularly mindful of the need for effective oversight of postal operations to insure that the postal services provided the public shall continue at an effective level and at reasonable rates. The failure of the Postal Service to provide the kind of extensive information which can sustain legislative and public confidence in the Postal Service, whether intentional or the result of oversight, must not continue. The provisions of section 2401 of title 39, requiring an annual report concerning the Postal Service's compliance with the public service policy of section 101 of title 39 has never been more than a simple recitation of the number of post offices in rural areas which have been opened, closed, or changed in status since the last report. The new reporting requirements go far beyond that kind of enumeration and, coupled with the requirement for appearances by officials of the Postal Service before the legislative committees responsible for oversight of postal affairs, will promote better administration of congressional policy, and better relations between the Executive and Legislative branches.[33]

Postal Rate Commission. Commissioners had been appointed by the President, but the 1976 amendments require them to be confirmed by the Senate. The amendments also allow a commissioner to continue after the term of office ends until a successor has been confirmed. In addition, the chairman was given certain executive authority to facilitate better administration of the commission.

An important time constraint was added to require the Postal Rate Commission to issue its recommended decisions on future rate cases (not mail classification cases) within ten months. Standards required at proceedings of the commission were relaxed to speed the hearing process. Proposed rates can no longer be put into effect temporarily if no action is taken on a request within ninety days. Rather, the Postal Service must wait ten months before temporary rates can be put into effect, and by then a recommended decision should be rendered by the Postal Rate Commission. However, the ninety-day waiting period still applies to mail classification cases.

A new criterion was also added to those the Postal Rate Commission considers in recommending rates: "the educational, cultural, scientific, and informational value to the recipient of mail matter." According to Section 3622 (b)(2) of the Postal Reorganization Act, high "cultural, education and informational values" to the recipient of second-class mail were to be used by the Postal Service to justify *low* rates for that mail class.[34] But the chief examiner found inconsistencies in Postal Service claims because high values to recipients were also used to justify high rates for first-class mail.[35] The new public service criterion will be difficult to evaluate and apply in Postal Rate Commission deliberations.

Commission on Postal Service. A seven-member commission was established by the 1976 amendments (three members appointed by the President, one postal employee and one other member chosen by the president pro tempore of the Senate, and like members chosen by the speaker of the House). The postmaster general and the chairman of the Postal Rate Commission were to serve as ex officio members without vote. The commission was to study postal problems generally and to study and issue recommendations in specified areas of interest as follows: (1) the public service aspects–identifying them, estimating their costs, and determining the extent they should be supported through appropriations; (2) the rate-making criteria of current law; (3) the levels of service and the extent to which appropriations should support various services; and (4) the long-range impact of electronic techniques on the Postal Service.

Several limitations were placed on Postal Service actions for the period between enactment of the 1976 amendments and the filing of the report of the Commission on Postal Service. No postal rate or fee was to be increased. Service also was to be maintained in all areas at least at the level provided on July 1, 1976. No post office could be closed during that period, unless patrons consented in writing.

Report of the Commission on Postal Service

The Commission on Postal Service consisted largely of persons having an interest in the present policies of the Postal Service. Of the seven appointed members, two represented employees of the Postal Service (a requirement of the 1976 amendments) and two others were affiliated in some way with magazines, which benefit from the current structure of postal rates. The report of the commission, when issued on April 18, 1977, found the Postal Service provided "comprehensive and generally acceptable levels of services at reasonable rates."[36] It contained modest suggestions, but no explanation or remedy for the recent problems in Postal Service performance.

The commission report urged that the Board of Governors be preserved, although it recommended that the Postal Rate Commission be given final authority for rate and classification decisions, subject only to judicial review. The commission recommended cuts in service in order to reduce costs (five-day-a-week delivery to addresses, for example), and an increase in the annual appropriation (to ten percent of postal expenses the previous year), in addition to a one-time $625 million appropriation to eliminate indebtedness. Dependability of timely delivery was emphasized as a desirable service goal, and electronic communications were to be investigated by the Postal Service for possible mail-service use. The commission opposed any relaxation of the private express statutes.

One surprising commission recommendation was to limit to 60 percent the fraction of total cost that could be attributed to individual classes of mail.[37] What is surprising is that this recommendation is based, not on any evidence that the attribution of more cost to individual classes of mail is not appropriate, but on the consequences that might result from higher rates that would follow greater cost attribution:

> After postal reorganization, as rates increased [parcel post], volume dropped from 536 million pieces in 1971 to 338 million in 1976; revenue dropped from $668 million to $447 million.[38]
>
> Several important conclusions can be drawn from these developments. The ability of users of all classes of mail to absorb rate increases and continue to increase mail volume is no longer a valid assumption. Shifting institutional costs to attributable costs and requiring the subordinate classes to assume a greater rate burden will further erode total mail volume.

This plea that only a limited percentage of costs should be attributed to classes of mail is essentially the position taken repeatedly by the Postal Service in rate cases. In such proceedings it has always attributed a much smaller portion of total cost to mail classes than that attributed by any other party to the hearings.[39]

Evidence on the cost question itself does not seem to support the Postal Service position. In individual post offices,[40] and in the entire postal system,[41] costs actually respond so much to changes in mail volume that no large fraction of total costs can be independent of mail volume as the Postal Service has asserted. That more cost can be attributed to mail classes than the Postal Service attributes to them was also amply demonstrated by the Office of the Commission and by the chief administrative law judge in his initial decision in Postal Rate Commission Docket R74-1.

In addition to preventing the arbitrary attribution of postal costs to the classes of mail that cause them, the commission recommended a list of factors to be considered in apportioning the remaining costs to various classes of mail. Included among these factors are some of the provisions that guide rate setting under current law, plus one new one that has been used by Postal Service in rate cases, namely, "the relative demand for each class or subclass of mail or type of mail service." These collected provisions will be listed below, because they are included in a major House bill (H.R. 7700) under current consideration. By limiting the scope for tracing the genuine causes of cost and raising the importance of other factors, these provisions would give to postal authorities great discretion in deciding costs and consequently in setting rates. In preventing by statute the full attribution of postal costs, the recommendations also may prevent the Postal Service from complying with Section 403(c) of the Postal Reorganization Act.

> In providing services and in establishing classifications, rates, and fees under this title, the Postal Service shall not, except as specifically authorized in this title, make any undue or unreasonable discrimination among users of the mails, nor shall it grant any undue or unreasonable preferences to any such user.[42]

Other studies of Postal Service performance have resulted in recommendations quite different from those of the Commission on Postal Service. The Department of Justice strongly criticizes cross subsidization of rates by the Postal Service. It also calls for careful study of the private express statutes, since their repeal would tend to prevent cross subsidization.[43] The Council on Wage and Price Stability strongly urged the repeal of the express statutes.[44] As noted above, the diagnoses in appellate court decisions and in the initial decision of the chief examiner in Docket R74-1 indicate that even today the costing and pricing of postal services do not comply with the provisions of the 1970 Postal Reorganization Act.

MAJOR ISSUES

A major objective of the Postal Reorganization Act was to provide that those who use the service should pay its costs.[45] It was intended that the Postal Service be self-sufficient except for a transitional period when "phasing" appropriations would cushion the shock of higher rates on some business users.[46] The continuation of reduced-rate mail was to depend on congressional appropriations.[47]

It was recognized that far-reaching improvements in efficiency would have to be achieved before a self-sufficient Postal Service could be a reality, a goal which the House Post Office and Civil Service Committee recognized could not be realized much before 1978.[48] Such improvements in efficiency were not achieved so quickly, as can be seen above, in the section Experience under the Act.

However, the Postal Service continues to be subject to the Postal Reorganization Act requirement "that each class of mail or type of mail service bear the direct and indirect postal costs attributable to that class or type plus that portion of all other costs of the Postal Service reasonably assignable to such class or type. Knowledge of the costs properly allocable to each class of mail or type of mail service is vital to responsible evaluation of rates and fees, whether self-sufficiency is attained or not.

In debate on the 1976 amendments, Congressman Don Clausen (R-Calif.) specifically charged that the Postal Service historically has set low parcel post rates in order to undercut competing private carriers.[49] He claimed that the difference between the cost of parcel post deliveries to the Postal Service and the rate charged users has been paid by higher first-class rates. First-class rates do not have to stand the test of competition because of the Postal Service's monopoly with respect to the delivery of such mail.[50]

One issue that emerges from this history is whether the Postal Service has complied with terms of the Postal Reorganization Act in setting rates. Another question is just how to provide the persistent congressional review needed to assure that the Postal Service is performing adequately. Where control over such matters as rates and levels of service should rest commands continuing attention. Another often raised question is how much subsidy, if any, should be provided for postal operations.

Cross Subsidization

Hearings on compliance with the Postal Reorganization Act were held in 1973 before the Senate Committee on Post Office and Civil Service. The chairman of the committee, Senator Gale W. McGee (D-Wyo.), said in opening the hearings:

> I would like to make it clear that I for one have no interest in conducting an inquisition into the Postal Service; threatening to "take back" the Postal Service—whatever that means; or substituting my judgment of how an executive agency should operate for the judgment of those who are presently held responsible. It is my intention to inquire into the operations of the Postal Service for the sole purpose of determining whether the service is conducting its business in compliance with congressional policy. That is the proper function of the Congress—to declare what the policy of the United States shall be and to authorize or direct the appropriate officers of the executive branch to execute that policy.[51]

The hearings revealed that the Postal Service had not met major objectives of the Postal Reorganization Act. On the Postal Service side there were arguments that the aims were overly ambitious, but that progress toward them was being made.[52]

On the other side are serious charges by responsible evaluators, such as the Postal Rate Commission hearing examiner or chief administrative law judge in the first two postal rate cases, and the appeals courts in two subsequent appeals. These all held that rates set by the Postal Service were not in compliance with the Postal Reorganization Act, mainly because cost information was inadequate. The results of these inadequacies could be continuing financial problems for the Postal Service, because some services are priced below their costs. Chief Administrative Law Judge Seymour Wenner remarked in his initial opinion in Docket R74-1:

> When costs are more carefully attributed to classes of mail we find that these rates set by the Postal Service are below costs of service in many classes. This subsidy is paid principally by first-class mailers.
>
> . . .The Postal Service has become a tax-collecting agency, collecting money from first-class mailers to distribute to other favored classes.[53]

In the first two rate cases only about half of the total cost of postal operations was attributed to classes of mail. In the third case the Postal Rate Commission put about 60 percent of total cost in the category of attributable costs, and in its most recent rate proposal, which is now before the Postal Rate Commission, more than 70 percent of total cost is said to be attributed to classes of mail.

Congressional Review

Congressmen cannot leave the Postal Service alone because constituents with postal service problems will not leave them alone. Some congressmen wish to return budgetary control to Congress so that they can honor the responsibility they feel to their constituents who complain of mail problems. As Representative Bill Alexander (D-Ark.) put it:

> In [the Postal Service] we have a major Federal Agency created by Congress, the second largest employer of Federal employees, spending huge sums of taxpayers' money, performing a vital Government service without which the country could not exist; yet, incredibly, not having any of its top management personnel accountable in any way to the people or their elected representatives.[54]

Currently congressmen can seek information from the Postal Service about its methods, performance, or other matters. The 1976 amendments added more reporting requirements.

Senator Ernest F. Hollings (D-S.C.), a member of the Senate Post Office and Civil Service Committee, has expressed the view that the Postal Service had operated with little or no congressional oversight in six years, and that only "constant oversight by Congress can make the service sound and responsive."[55] In considering the 1976 amendments, members of Congress favored different approaches to the issue of congressional review and control.

H.R. 8603, as reported by the House Post Office and Civil Service Committee in 1975, attempted through periodic rather than regular authorizations of appropriations to make up deficits to "give Congress a greater role in determining the proper direction of postal policy without returning the Postal Service to the immense legislative and political restrictions placed on its predecessor prior to 1970."[56] It was felt that what "public service" is, for purposes of congressional subsidy, should be determined not by the Postal Service but rather by Congress.[57] However, this version of the bill did not impose additional requirements for reports to Congress.

The House bill also required Senate confirmation of the postmaster general. The Senate version of the bill and the version of the conference committee which was adopted by both houses omitted this change, relying on the special Commission on the Postal Service to study the issue and make recommendations.

During floor debate in the House, Representative Alexander proposed an amendment which was adopted over the objection of the leadership of the House Post Office and Civil Service Committee. Representative Alexander argued that the amendment "restores accountability of the U.S. Postal Service to the people by requiring the Postal Service to come to Congress each year for authorization and for appropriation of its budget."[58] Postal revenues would be deposited in the general fund of the Treasury, thereby ending for practical purposes the Postal Service's operation independent of the usual annual appropriations process. Representative Alexander stated this would insure that postal management would be responsive to Congress without abolishing the Postal Service and recreating the U.S. Post Office Department.

Representative James M. Hanley (D-N.Y.), chairman of the Postal Service Subcommittee, opposed the amendment for the following reasons: it would pull the rug from under the Postal Reorganization Act; it would leave the Postal Rate Commission without any purpose; it would take the challenge away from the Postal Service; and it would obligate the taxpayers to make up every dollar of the postal deficit.[59]

The Alexander amendment passed the House but was not included in the Senate version of the bill or in the version of the conference committee. The conference substituted the principle expressed in the special requirements for reporting to Congress contained in the Senate bill. It also required that the officers of the Postal Service appear before the substantive committees of the House and Senate before March 15 of each year to testify and respond to questions.[60]

Control of Rates

Under the Postal Reorganization Act no agency was set up to oversee postal rates in the way regulatory commissions oversee pricing in other economic activities. The Postal Rate Commission was only to recommend decisions to the Board of Governors of the Postal Service, where ultimate control was lodged. The Postal Service also controls the budget of the Postal Rate Commission, although the President appoints its members.

The Postal Reorganization Act Amendments of 1976 made the President's appointments to the Postal Rate Commission subject to Senate confirmation; they set a time limit of ten months for reaching recommended decisions; they modified several administrative arrangements; and they added the new criterion of "educational, cultural, scientific, and informational value to the recipient of mail matter" to rate-making considerations. However, no major change was made in *where* control over rate making would reside.

The Commission on Postal Service urged that final authority for rate decisions rest with the Postal Rate Commission, without review by the Board of Governors but subject to judicial review, and that funds for the commission be appropriated by Congress.[61] Although the Commission on Postal Service recommended reducing the power of the Board of Governors, it nevertheless recommended that the board be retained:

> In the past two years, increasing pressure has developed to eliminate the Board of Governors and return to Presidential appointment of the Postmaster General and Deputy Postmaster General. One reason given is that the Postal Service and the Postmaster General have experienced difficulty since reorganization in securing the attention and approval of the Administration, particularly regarding increased financial support. This difficulty led critics to suggest that the Postmaster General would be more successful if he were a member of the President's Cabinet, or at least a member of the President's official family.
>
> We do not agree. There is no evidence that the Postal Service's financial condition would be changed if the Postmaster General were appointed by the President. A chief reason for the enactment of the Postal Reorganization Act was to remove the Post Office Department from Cabinet status because modernization and major capital improvements programs had not received priority consideration by the President or the Bureau of the Budget. The only time in the last half century when postal modernization received priority consideration was in the 1930's, when the Public Works Administration built post offices throughout the Nation as part of the national recovery effort. From that time until the late 1950's, practically no postal modernization and capital investment programs were undertaken. If the Postmaster General were returned to the "official family" of the President, we believe the opportunity for the Postal Service to carry out programs free from budgetary constraints and political pressure would be seriously jeopardized.[62]

The Kappel Commission had this to say about the proposal that the Postal Rate Commission's decisions should be subject only to review by Congress:

> Burdened with far more important responsibilities, Congress should not be asked to deal with the intricacies of postal rates. Rate-making and the development of new services are complex, interwoven responsibilities which need the detailed attention of experts in economics, accounting, marketing and engineering.[63]

The Postal Service prefers to retain its control over rates. E. T. Klassen, who then served as postmaster general, confirmed that view in the 1973 hearings:

> Congress has resolutely resisted all attempts to alter the guidelines of the Postal Reorganization Act and I earnestly hope that this attitude will continue. If every rate decision were subject to pressure by special interest groups and was contested and reexamined in Congress, we will have gained very little from Postal Reorganization.[64]

Another alternative was advanced by Representative Paul Simon (D-Ill.). During debate on the 1976 amendments he offered an amendment to abolish the Postal Rate Commission and tie postal rates to the consumer price index.[65] He quoted the postmaster general as saying the goal has been to keep rates at or below a level consistent with the growth of the consumer price index. Representative Simon and certain other members felt the Postal Rate Commission performed no useful function. Representative Cardiss Collins (D-Ill.) said the commission was set up as a buffer, but that it does not serve as a buffer. Thus, these House members would bypass unduly lengthy postal rate proceedings in favor of indexed rates. Postal officials are understood to believe the Postal Rate Commission does perform a buffer function.

In opposition to this proposal, Representative Hanley argued that the consumer price index was not the proper vehicle to use in complicated rate-making proceedings.[66] Representative Edward Derwinski (R-Ill.) argued that abolishing the commission would put Congress back into fixing personnel costs, which Congress had tried to avoid. He argued in effect that rate increases would have to be more generous than the index to cover the generosity of Congress to employees.[67] He dreaded to think how the House and Senate galleries would be packed by uniformed postal workers looking down as Congress decided what their next pay increase would be. The indexing proposal for rates was not adopted.

Service Level Control

Many members of Congress feel that Congress should control the level of service to postal patrons, at least in broad outline. It is argued that broad cutbacks in service have met substantial opposition from the public and Congress and that the impact on total postal costs would not be great.[68]

> Major cost reductions could be realized, but even so they would not produce the savings necessary to eliminate the need for rate increases. . . .
>
> A reduction in delivery services from 6 days to 5 would result in savings of approximately $350 million. It has been estimated by the Comptroller General that a reduction in the number of third-class offices from 12,000 to 6,000 and the elimination of more than 6,000 fourth-class offices could save approximately $130 million. If delivery to remote places, now generally made 6 days a week, were reduced uniformly to 2 days, savings of $400 million could be realized. . . .It is questionable if such policies, if effected, would fulfill the mandate of Congress, which has directed the Postal Service to "provide prompt, reliable, and efficient services to patrons in all areas," and to "render postal services to all communities."[69]

Senate McGee, chairman of the Senate Post Office and Civil Service Committee, stated the Postal Service saved $2 million a year by closing 186 small post offices, a sum that would run the postal service for just nine minutes. However, in doing this, the service angered fifty-three members of Congress, provoked a lawsuit, and persuaded many that in yet another public area the quality of life is diminishing, according to Senator McGee.[70]

On the other hand, management has to have some flexibility to achieve "sensible economies given the long-term financial realities that must be faced."[71] Thus, the Postal Service opposed the congressional attempt to require delivery to the door at new addresses, except as provided by local authorities.[72] Such requirements would be very difficult to administer and could limit innovation.[73]

Subsidy

The extent of postal subsidy, if there is to be any, has been a question continually at issue in the 1970s. Representative Hanley has urged an explicit annual subsidy of $35 per delivery address (a total of about $2.6 billion).[74] Against the argument that Congress should control postal operations more directly by requiring congressional approval of postal appropriations, he points out the undesirable incentive this would give the Postal Service to bring a bill for services and say: "Pay it, taxpayers."[75] The incentive consequences of alternative subsidy arrangements certainly are important, but to create any incentive, advance knowledge of the basis for the subsidy award is needed.[76]

The argument for subsidy is usually tied to some public service aspect of postal service. Without pinning these services down precisely, the Commission on Postal Service recommended that public service appropriations be set each year at 10 percent of postal expenses in the preceding year. A one-time appropriation of $625 million was also recommended.[77]

Representative David N. Henderson (D-N.C.), chairman of the House Post Office and Civil Service Committee, argued that postal rates must increase if costs rise. However, he did not feel mail users "should pay all of the costs which result from inflation and other factors over which mail users have no control."[78] It is also argued that rate increases tend to reduce postal volume, which may have an adverse effect on revenues.[79]

The Postal Service takes the position that a subsidy requires taxpayers to assume the burden for a charge which should be borne mostly by the mailers who have the benefit of the service.[80] In the most recent development, W. Bowman Cutter, executive assistant director of the Office of Management and Budget testified for the Carter administration on September 20, 1977, that the administration opposes increased subsidies.[81] The proposal for subsidies set at 15 percent of the previous year's postal budget was opposed on the ground this would remove incentives to cut costs and improve efficiency. The witness argued that with scarce resources and infinite demands for money, new money for the Postal Service should come from higher rates and increased efficiency.

LEGISLATIVE PROPOSALS

Major House and Senate Bills

S. 1692 and H.R. 7700 are major bills to be considered. H.R. 7700 was introduced in the House June 9 by Representatives Hanley and Charles H. Wilson (D-Calif.). S. 1692 was introduced in the Senate June 14 by Senator John Melcher (D-Mont.), Senator Quentin N. Burdick (D-N. Dak.), and Senator George McGovern (D-S. Dak.). These two bills are similar in the way they would (1) modify the organization of the Postal Service, (2) provide routine congressional oversight of major investment decisions of the Postal Service, (3) have the Postal Rate Commission budget sent via the President (for recommendations only) to Congress (rather than to the Postal Service for adjustment and payment from the Postal Service Fund), (4) maintain the frequency of mail delivery at current levels, and (5) explicitly deny that any provisions are to affect current collective bargaining agreements or the collective bargaining process.

In the important area of procedures for adjusting rates or fees or appropriations, the bills differ. They also differ in the issue of post office closings and consolidations. The House bill also deals with size and weight limits for other than letter mail, with the question of allowing Postal Service rather than Justice Department lawyers to represent the Postal Service, and with the applicability of federal law to the disposal of old surplus property.

Additional Bills

H.R. 19, introduced January 4, 1977, by Representative Wilson, contains provisions to change the organization of the Postal Service, procedures to handle operating deficits, including requests for appropriations from Congress, provisions for review of capital expenditures, procedures for handling Postal Rate Commission budgets, and a statement regarding collective bargaining agreements. Most of these provisions were essentially carried over into H.R. 7700 or S. 1692.

S. 201, introduced January 12 by Senator Burdick, would establish an arbitration board to settle disputes between the Postal Service and other organizations. H.R. 679, introduced January 4 by Representative Patricia Schroeder (D-Colo.), would have the President rather than the Board of Governors appoint the postmaster general, with the advice and consent of the Senate, but it would retain in the Board of Governors the power to remove the postmaster general. It would not abolish the Board of Governors, as is provided in H.R. 7700 and S. 1692.

On January 10, 1977, Senator Hollings introduced S. 94, which would return the finances of the Postal Service to congressional control by requiring annual appropriations that the Postal Service would have to justify. There would be limited rights to issue debt obligations. Under this bill the Postal Rate Commission would still function but the Board of Governors of the Postal Service would be abolished. The postmaster general would be appointed by the President and confirmed by the Senate.

H.R. 5549, introduced March 23, 1977, by Representative Alexander, would put postal revenues in the Treasury's general fund, rather than appropriate them automatically to the Postal Service as under current law, and would require the Postal Service to request congressional appropriations to carry out its purposes and functions for fiscal years 1978 and 1979.

Three other House bills–H.R. 3012, introduced February 2, 1977, by Representative Charles B. Rangel (D-N.Y.); H.R. 3055, introduced February 2, 1977, by Representative David E. Satterfield, III (D-Va.); and H.R. 4613, introduced March 8, 1977, by Representative Alexander–would all repeal the Postal Reorganization Act and reenact the provisions it replaced, returning the Post Office to its status as an executive department.

Similar Provisions in H.R. 7700 and S. 1692

Postal Organization. Both H.R. 7700 and S. 1692 abolish the Board of Governors and give executive responsibility for directing and controlling the expenditures of the Postal Service to the postmaster general. Both bills call for the President to appoint the postmaster general with the advice and consent of the Senate. The postmaster general would also be given many powers now held by the Board of Governors. However, the two bills differ in the authority they give to the postmaster general relative to the Postal Rate Commission. That question is treated below in the section Adjustment of Rates.

Parts of H.R. 19 and H.R. 679 are included in these bills. S. 94 and H.R. 5549 would give greater financial control of postal operations to Congress, through the appropriations process, while H.R. 3012, H.R. 3035, and H.R. 4613 would return postal operations to a government department as it was before the Postal Reorganization Act was passed in 1970.

The administration's witness has testified in favor of retention of the Board of Governors and continuation of the autonomous Postal Service. The administration favors presidential appointment of the postmaster general, as do the authors of H.R. 7700 and S. 1692.[82] However, the administration would provide for six-year terms for the postmaster general whereas the pending bills would not.

Capital Investments. Neither H.R. 7700 nor S. 1692 would allow a capital investment with total estimated costs above $200 million to be undertaken without an opportunity for congressional review. A report describing and justifying such an investment would have to be submitted to both the Post Office and Civil Service Committee of the House and the Committee on Governmental Affairs of the Senate. Work could not begin on the project until recommendations had been received from both committees. The bills call for the committees to review any such proposed investment, to hold hearings as considered necessary, and to return recommendations within four months of the time a report proposing the investment is received.

Postal Rate Commission Budget. Both bills would have the Postal Rate Commission (the independent agency established to recommend decisions to the Board of Governors regarding rates, fees, and mail classes) submit a budget to the President, rather than to the Postal Service as at present. The President could make recommendations (but not revisions) and pass the budget on to Congress for action. Under the Postal Reorganization Act, the Postal Service now provides funds for the Postal Rate Commission from its Postal Service Fund.

Frequency of Delivery. Both bills require that 1977 delivery frequencies be maintained, although they use different dates to define the 1977 frequencies. S. 1692 would set the delivery frequencies prevailing on April 21 as a minimum level, while H.R. 7700 chooses those in effect on June 1. The Carter administration has since taken the position that decisions on frequency of deliveries should be left to the postmaster general.[83]

Collective Bargaining Agreements. Neither bill would affect any collective bargaining agreement already in effect, nor would they affect the process of collective bargaining in the future. (The only provision of S. 201 is for an arbitration board to settle disputes.)

Adjustment of Rates

Senate Version. Under the Postal Reorganization Act (Section 3625) the Board of Governors has power to reject a recommended decision of the Postal Rate Commission. The board can also modify recommended rates, if those recommended by the commission are inadequate, so that total estimated income plus appropriations will equal total estimated cost. Under S. 1692, that power would go to the postmaster general.

S. 1692 would also add a new section called Appropriations or Adjustments for Operating Deficits. The new section provides that, if the Postal Service finds its estimated revenues insufficient to cover its estimated costs for a fiscal year, it has three options. It can (1) ask Congress for an appropriation to make up the difference, (2) request that the Postal Rate Commission submit a recommended decision (under Section 3622(a)) for modified rates or fees, or (3) seek an advisory opinion from the Postal Rate Commission regarding a change in the nature of postal services (under Section 3661(b)).

These three options are not available as entirely separate and independent actions. If the Postal Service asks for an appropriation from Congress, it must also report to the Postal Rate Commission all implications for changes in rates and fees or changes in postal services, in the event Congress does not appropriate the amount requested. Similarly, if the Postal Service suggests to the Postal Rate Commission certain changes in rates or fees or in postal services, it must also provide Congress with an analysis showing the size of appropriation that, when added to estimated revenues, could defray all estimated costs. These provisions are included to save time, while allowing for alternative corrective actions within certain specified time limits.

The possibilities of alternative corrective actions are spelled out according to the following timetable. If the Postal Service asks Congress for an appropriation and after five months has not been granted the full amount requested (and has not approached the Postal Rate Commission), it may make a request of the Postal Rate Commission. Regarding a request for changes in rates or fees (under Section 3622 (a)), the commission is to reach its recommended decision within the next five months. Also, the commission is to take into account any appropriation Congress did in fact make. If, instead of the foregoing, the Postal Service initially had sought a change in rates or fees, the Postal Rate Commission is not to issue a recommended decision for five months, allowing Congress that much time to appropriate the needed sum or a part of it, and the Postal Rate Commission must take this sum into account in its recommended decision. However, if the Postal Service initially had sought an advisory opinion on changes in postal services, there is again a five-month period in which the changes cannot take effect. If Congress appropriates funds during that time, the Postal Service's proposal is to be modified accordingly.

House Version. Under H.R. 7700 the postmaster general would not take over the power of the Board of Governors to modify rates recommended by the Postal Rate Commission. The power to set rates and fees would be lodged in the Postal Rate Commission, although Congress could express disapproval and prevent new rates from going into effect. This is very much like the authority for the Postal Rate Commission, with a congressional check, that was originally proposed by the Kappel Commission.[84] Under a new Subsection 3624(e), the Postal Rate Commission's final decision would take effect if and only if (1) the commission delivers a copy of its final decision to the Senate and the House and (2) after sixty working days Congress has not adopted a "concurrent resolution of disapproval" of the final decision. Another proposed Subsection (2401(j)) would authorize appropriations to cover the reduction in estimated revenues following the adoption by Congress of a concurrent resolution of disapproval.

The House bill also proposes revisions to the centrally important sections of the Postal Reorganization Act regarding rates and fees. The revisions are those recommended by the Commission on Postal Service. A clearer definition of total estimated costs is given in the bill, particularly in the precision with which the provision for contingencies is stated. The most important departures from the Postal Reorganization Act occur in the guidelines the Postal Rate Commission is to follow in setting rates and fees under the terms of Subsection 3622(b). Included in H.R. 7700 is a definition of *attributable cost* which agrees nominally with the measure adhered to by the Postal Service, and there is also the arbitrary upper limit for attributable cost that was recommended by the Commission on Postal Service at 60 percent of the total cost.

The proposed guidelines compare with current provisions as follows:

Proposed H.R. 7700 Subsection 3622(b)[85]	**Postal Reorganization Act Subsection 3622(b)**
(b)(1) Upon receiving any proposal from the Postal Service, the Commission shall make a decision on the request for changes in rates or fees in each class or subclass of mail or type of service in accordance with the policies of this title and the requirements of this subsection.	(b) Upon receiving a request, the Commission shall make a recommended decision on the request for changes in rates or fees in each class of mail or type of service in accordance with the policies of this title and the following factors:
(2) Each class or subclass of mail or type of service shall bear those postal costs attributable to that class, subclass, or type because the costs vary with the volume of that class or subclass or type of service. Attributable costs shall be those costs which vary with volume over 3 years or less. If attributable costs exceed 60 percent of total estimated costs, the attributable costs of the class, subclass, or type shall be reduced to an amount that is determined by multiplying the attributable costs of the class, subclass, or type by a fraction whose numerator is 60 and denominator is a whole number equal to the percentage of total estimated costs determined to be attributable.	(3) the requirement that each class of mail or type of mail service bear the direct and indirect postal costs attributable to that class or type plus that portion of all other costs of the Postal Service reasonably assignable to such class or type;

Proposed H.R. 7700 Subsection 3622(b)	Postal Reorganization Act Subsection 3622(b)
(3) The remaining costs not attributed under paragraph (2) of this subsection shall be apportioned, after deducting an estimated amount for public service appropriations, among each class or subclass of mail or type of service as a revenue burden on the basis of	
(3)(A) the quality and character of the mail service provided to both the sender and the recipient, including collection, speed of transmission, privacy, and priority of handling and delivery.	(2) the value of the mail service actually provided each class or type of mail service to both the sender and the recipient, including but not limited to the collection, mode of transportation, and priority of delivery;
(3)(B) the effect of the proposed rates on the general public, business mail users, and enterprises in the private sector of the economy engaged in the delivery of mail matter other than letters;	(4) the effect of rate increases upon the general public, business mail users, and enterprises in the private sector of the economy engaged in the delivery of mail matter other than letters;
(3)(C) the available alternative means of sending and receiving letters and other mail matter at reasonable costs.	(5) the available alternative means of sending and receiving letters and other mail matter at reasonable costs;
(3)(D) the educational, cultural, scientific, and informational benefit of the mail matter to the Nation.	(8) the educational, cultural, scientific, and informational value to the recipient of mail matter;
(3)(E) the relative demand for each class or subclass of mail or type of mail service.	
	(1) the establishment and maintenance of a fair and equitable schedule;
	(6) the degree of preparation of mail for delivery into the postal system performed by the mailer and its effect upon reducing costs to the Postal Service;

Proposed H.R. 7700 Subsection 3622(b)	Postal Reorganization Act Subsection 3622(b)
	(7) simplicity of structure for the entire schedule and simple, identifiable relationships between the rates or fees charged the various classes of mail for postal services;
	(9) and such other factors as the Commission deems appropriate.

These H.R. 7700 guidelines depart from the aim of the Postal Reorganization Act to have each class of mail (with certain exceptions for certain public service categories) pay all the costs attributable to it. Instead, the proposals essentially follow the manner of pricing before the Postal Reorganization Act was passed.

Appropriations to the Postal Service are authorized under the House bill, limited in fiscal 1979 and 1980 to 15 percent of total operating expenses in the previous year and not to continue after that (unless specifically authorized by later legislation). Funds thus appropriated are to support post offices which might not be deemed to be self-sustaining, to establish research and development programs equivalent to those of private communications businesses, and to continue the frequency of mail delivery in effect on June 1, 1977.

Administration Views

Based on Office of Management and Budget and Domestic Council recommendations submitted to the President, the Carter administration's witness testified on September 21, 1977, that the Postal Service should continue to operate as an autonomous businesslike agency subject only to presidential appointment of the postmaster general.[86] The basic reforms launched with the Postal Reorganization Act of 1970 were said to remain viable and sound.

Rather than additional subsidies, the administration supports the goal of a self-sufficient Postal Service by 1984, without new subsidy. Congressional veto of postal increases was opposed. A subsidy based on a specified percentage of the postal budget was opposed on the ground that this would remove incentives to cut costs and improve efficiency.

Other Issues

Closing of Post Offices. H.R. 7700 requires that before post offices are closed or consolidated, the Postal Service is to conduct hearings during a sixty-day period in the area that is to be affected. S. 1692 would forbid the closing of any office serving thirty-five or more families from March 15, 1977, to December 31, 1979, if it was in service on July 1, 1976. During that period, even post offices serving less than thirty-five families are to be kept in service unless the written consent of 60 percent of regular patrons over eighteen years of age is obtained.

The Carter administration apparently would leave decisions as to post office closings to the postmaster general.[87]

Legal Representation. Under the Postal Reorganization Act, the Justice Department either furnishes legal representation for the Postal Service or gives prior consent to the Postal Service's arranging for its own representation. With respect to cases arising under chapter 36 of Title 39, United States Code, which has to do with the Postal Rate Commission, Rates and Fees and Mail Classes, and Postal Services and Complaints, H.R. 7700 would allow the Postal Service to represent itself in litigation without approval by the Justice Department, either through its own attorneys or through attorneys whose services are obtained by contract. This procedure was recommended by the Commission on Postal Service.[88]

A reorganization study of the Carter administration is focusing on the use of lawyers and agency representation. No conclusions have been announced.

Size and Weight Limits. Under existing law the maximum combined length and girth of other than letter mail is 84 inches, and the maximum weight is forty pounds, with 100 inches and seventy pounds allowed in specified cases. H.R. 7700 would raise those limits generally to 100 inches and seventy pounds, with minor qualifications added to ensure consistency across mail classes, as the Commission on Postal Service recommended.[89]

Surplus Property. H.R. 7700 would subject the Postal Service to federal law in chapter 10 of Title 40 of the United States Code, relating to management and disposal of property, which dates back to the forming of the Postal Service under the Postal Reorganization Act.

POSTAL SERVICE PROSPECTS

The Postal Service is an enormous organization that fulfills important responsibilities day after day. Since the 1960s it has faced persistent service problems and financial difficulties which the Congress has attempted to remedy by legislation, the most important of which was the Postal Reorganization Act of 1970. That act was intended to remove postal service from politics in order that sound management methods could be used and cross subsidization ended. This practice favors some classes of mail with low rates while others bear the excess costs. The price discrimination that lies behind cross subsidization may cause deficits and the need for an overall subsidy, because those who pay low rates use more of the services that cause the deficits, while those who pay high rates reduce their use of the profitable services.

A major issue is whether to enforce the requirement that postal rates for various services must cover their costs. If that aim of the Postal Reorganization Act is abandoned, the subsidies to different services would inevitably require the attention of Congress, as would various other questions of service and investment. The Postal Reorganization Act recommended that rates cover costs as a key step in enforcing efficiency and responsiveness. To comply, the Postal Service would have to satisfy users of the mail service in order to win their patronage.

Much debate, both before and after passage of the Postal Reorganization Act, has focused on whether certain services, particularly the transmission of cultural and educational materials, should be subsidized.[90] Section 3622(b)(3) of the act itself was quite clear on this point:

> Each class of mail or type of mail service [shall] bear the direct postal costs attributable to that class or type plus that portion of all other costs of the Postal Service reasonably assignable to that class or type.[91]

Section 403(c) of the act provides:

> The Postal Service shall not, except as specifically authorized in this title, make any undue or unreasonable discrimination among users of the mails, nor shall it grant any undue or unreasonable preferences to such user.[92]

Each class of mail was to recover in rates at least those costs that could be either attributed or reasonably assigned to it. The Postal Service may still lack the cost information to meet these requirements, but its most recent rate proposal indicates that greater reliance is now being placed on estimates of the costs of providing services.

H.R. 3012, H.R. 3035, and H.R. 4613 would retreat from the cost coverage requirement of the Postal Reorganization Act and return to the practices of the pre-1970 Post Office Department.

By eliminating the Board of Governors of the Postal Service, H.R. 7700 and S. 1692 would remove the anomaly of a Postal Rate Commission, presumably an expert body prepared to apply the law in rate-making and classification matters, being subject to the Postal Service's top management, the Board of Governors. Both bills remove control over Postal Rate Commission budgets from the Postal Service, and budget requests would go to Congress through the President instead. H.R. 7700 would give control over rates and classification to the Postal Rate Commission (subject to review by Congress), but S. 1692 would strengthen Postal Service control by giving the postmaster general the power to reject Postal Rate Commission decisions. The Carter administration would retain the Board of Governors as the final authority on postal matters.

The House bill gives more rate-making power to the Postal Rate Commission. However, it also alters the applicable rate-making principles to reduce reliance on the cost of services in setting rates and increases the discretion of the rate-setting body. The proposed rate-making guidelines are those recommended by the Commission on Postal Service, which include an arbitrary limit of 60 percent on the portion of total cost that is to be attributed to classes of mail, a limit which would be exceeded by the most recent Postal Service rate proposals.

The pending bills move toward mandated levels of service and a greater invitation to subsidy from tax revenues. On the other hand, the administration has recently sounded its support for continued autonomy for the Postal Service, subject only to the President's appointment of the postmaster general.

Debate on the 1976 amendments often took a pessimistic view of the potential of the new Postal Service, though there was an expressed reluctance to reinsert Congress in the role of deciding postal pay raises. Much discussion was devoted to heavy postal deficits and a claimed lack of sensitivity by the service.

On the other hand, the Postal Service is reducing employment levels by attrition and is making a greater effort to attribute costs realistically by class of mail. The administration has given a vote of confidence to the concept of a "businesslike" Postal Service, which will decide on levels of service, on post office closings, and on rate increases other than for the first-class rate for individuals, and will make the service self-sufficient by 1984. It claims pending rate increases will bring in $2 billion a year in additional revenues.[93]

Increased postal volume has cut the postal deficit for the most recent year. There will be concern whether increased rates will stunt the growth of postal volume.

Postal officials can take solace from the fact that the costs and rates of their competitors are also rising.

The fate of an agency which touches so many lives deserves and no doubt will receive the closest scrutiny.

NOTES TO TEXT

[1]George L. Priest, "The History of the Postal Monopoly in the United States," *Journal of Law and Economics*, vol. 13 (1973), p. 48.

[2]U.S. Constitution, art. I, sec. 8, cl. 7.

[3]Priest, "The History of the Postal Monopoly in the United States," pp. 52-55.

[4]See 5 Stat. 732 (March 3, 1845).

[5]84 Stat. 719 (August 12, 1970).

[6]Kappel Commission, *Towards Postal Excellence, The Report of the President's Commission on Postal Organization* (Washington, D.C.: Government Printing Office, June 1968).

[7]The extension was provided in 88 Stat. 287 (June 30, 1974).

[8]Senate Report 94-966.

[9]This $920 million was 10 percent of the sum appropriated to the Post Office Department for fiscal 1971. The appropriation was to be maintained at that same level each year through 1979, after which it would gradually be lowered to half that amount in 1984, and remain thereafter at that level. See 39 U.S.C. 2401.

[10]39 U.S.C. 101.

[11]*Congressional Record*, vol. 122 (August 23, 1976), p. S14266, statement of Senator Gale W. McGee, chairman of the Senate Post Office and Civil Service Committee.

[12]Senate Report 94-966, p. 4.

[13]Ibid.

[14]Ibid., letter dated March 18, 1976, from Louis A. Cox, general counsel of the U.S. Postal Service to Senator Gale McGee, chairman of the Senate Committee on Post Office and Civil Service.

[15]*Congressional Record*, vol. 122 (August 23, 1976), p. S14272, statement of Senator Hiram L. Fong, ranking minority member of the Senate Post Office and Civil Service Committee.

[16]Senator Report 94-966, p. 7.

[17]*Electronic Message Systems for the U.S. Postal Service* (Washington, D.C.: National Academy of Science, 1976). See also the criticism of Postal Service technology by Jacob Rabinow in Postal Rate Commission Docket R74-1 at 17/2873-2972.

[18]Commission on Postal Service, *Report of the Commission on Postal Service*, April 18, 1977, vol. 1, p. 11.

[19]Associated Press news release as published in the *Washington Star,* September 10, 1977, p. A-3.

[20]*Report of the Commission on Postal Service,* April 18, 1977, vol. 1, p. 20.

[21]*Congressional Record,* vol. 121 (September 29, 1975), p. H9226, statement of Congressman David N. Henderson, chairman of the House Committee on Post Office and Civil Service.

[22]House Conference Report 94-1444.

[23]Senate Report 94-966, p. 4.

[24]Ibid., p. 6; in House debate Congressman Bill Alexander detailed $19,725,000 in cost overruns.

[25]Senate Report 94-966, p. 6.

[26]Chief Administrative Law Judge's Initial Decision on Postal Rate and Fees Increases, Postal Rate Commission Docket R74-1, vol. 1 (May 28, 1975), pp. 110-15.

[27]National Association of Greeting Card Publishers v. U.S. Postal Service (D.C. Cir., December 28, 1976).

[28]Association of American Publishers, Inc. v. Governors, U.S. Postal Service, 485 F. 2d 768 (D.C. Cir. 1973); and National Association of Greeting Card Publishers v. U.S. Postal Service (D.C. Cir. 1976).

[29]Ibid., slip opinion, pp. 41, 44, and 45.

[30]Chief Administrative Law Judge's Initial Decision on Postal Rate and Fee Increases, Postal Rate Commission Docket R74-1, vol. 1 (May 28, 1975), pp. 112-15, and Appendix I.

[31]*Report of the Commission on Postal Service,* April 18, 1977, vol. 1, p. 11.

[32]Senate Report 94-421; Public Law 94-421, 90 Stat. 1303 (September 10, 1976).

[33]House Conference Report 94-1444.

[34]See Postal Service testimony in Postal Rate Commission Docket R71-1 at 23/2789-91.

[35]Analysis of the Postal Service argument is presented in Chief Examiner's Initial Decision on Postal Rate and Fee Increases, Postal Rate Commission Docket R71-1, February 3, 1972, pp. 77-78.

[36]Senate Report 94-966.

[37]*Report of the Commission on Postal Service,* April 18, 1977, vol. 1, p. 64.

[38]Ibid., pp. 62-63.

[39]In Postal Rate Commission Docket R74-1, compare U.S.P.S. Exhibit 8 (as corrected) with O.O.C. Exhibit 201 (Supp.) Revised, p. 1, and Exhibit 222, p. 1.

[40]See Leonard Merewitz, "Costs and Returns to Scale in U.S. Post Offices," *Journal of the American Statistical Association,* September 1971, pp. 504-9; Fred Dziadek, "The Productivity of the U.S. Post Office: An Intertemporal and Cross-Sectional Study of Post Office Labor Productivity" (Ph.D. diss., Johns Hopkins University, 1959); Edmund H. Mantell, "Factors Affecting Labor Productivity in Post Offices," *Journal of the American Statistical Association,* June 1974, pp. 303-9.

[41]See Morton S. Baratz, *The Economics of the Postal Service* (Washington, D.C.: Public Affairs Press, 1962); U.S. Bureau of the Budget, *Measuring Productivity of Federal Government Organizations,* Washington, D.C., 1964; Rodney E. Stevenson, "Postal Pricing Problems and Production Functions" (Ph.D. diss., Michigan State University, 1973); and George M. Wattles, "The Rates and Costs of the United States Postal Service," *Journal of Law and Economics,* April 1963, pp. 89-117; or even the Post Office Department's *Summary Report of Cost System Task Force on Incremental Costs* (Washington, D.C.: Bureau of Finance and Administration, May 1970).

[42]84 Stat. 719, 723 (1970).

[43]Department of Justice, *Changing the Private Express Laws,* Washington, D.C., January 1977.

[44]Comments of the Council on Wage and Price Stability Concerning the Private Express Statutes, Postal Rate Commission Docket R76-4, January 16, 1976.

[45]*Congressional Record,* vol. 121 (September 29, 1975), p. H9227, statement of Congressman Brock Adams, chairman of the House Budget Committee.

[46]Ibid.

[47]House Report 91-1104.

[48]Ibid.

[49]*Congressional Record,* vol. 121 (September 29, 1975), p. H9231.

[50]Senator Jesse Helms offered an amendment to the proposed Postal Reorganization Act Amendments of 1976 which would have eliminated the Postal Service's monopoly position. See *Congressional Record,* vol. 122 (August 24, 1976), p. S14442. Senator Helms, while acknowledging there would be a continuing need to subsidize rural mail delivery, argued that competition would encourage the Postal Service to meet its goals. He quoted the President's Council on Wage and Price Stability that this change would promote "allocative efficiency"; it might be expected to promote operational efficiencies within the Postal Service; and it would likely stimulate innovation and changes in postal technology and restrain increases in postal labor costs reflecting improved productivity.

Congressman James Hanley of the House Subcommittee on the Postal Service argued that repeal of the private express statutes to remove the Postal Service's monopoly position would result in private competitors skimming off the most profitable business, leaving the Postal Service with the unprofitable business in underpopulated areas. See *Congressional Record,* vol. 121 (September 29, 1975), p. H9236. He further argued the postal monopoly allows every postal patron to have equality of service regardless of location.

Congressman Philip M. Crane countered by arguing that private carriers are now skimming off much fourth-class (parcel post) business but the Postal Service continues to provide fourth-class service to rural areas. He argued that private carriers would deliver letters more efficiently and at lower cost. In addition, they would be paying taxes to the government to help underwrite the subsidies paid to the Postal Service.

Senator Gale McGee argued that repeal of the private express statutes would gut the Postal Service and cited President Washington's reference to the Postal Service as "a chain that binds the country together." For an additional study on this subject see John Haldi, *Postal Monopoly: An Assessment of the Private Express Statutes* (Washington, D.C.: American Enterprise Institute, 1974).

[51]U.S., Congress, Senate, Committee on Post Office and Civil Service, *Hearings on Postal Oversight,* 93rd Congress, 1st session, part 1, p. 1.

[52]Ibid., pp. 6-62; See also U.S. Postal Service, *Annual Report of the Postmaster General,* 1975, p. 3.

[53]Chief Administrative Law Judge's Initial Decision, Postal Rate Commission Docket R74-1, vol. 1 (May 28, 1975), pp. 12-13.

[54]*Congressional Record,* vol. 121 (September 29, 1975), p. H9237.

[55]Senate Report 94-966, supplemental views of Senator Ernest F. Hollings.

[56]House Report 95-391, p. 4.

[57]Ibid.

[58]*Congressional Record,* vol. 121 (September 29, 1975), p. H9238.

[59]Ibid., p. H9241.

[60]See Section 2 of Public Law 94-421 amending 39 U.S.C. 2401; House Conference Report 94-1444, Joint Explanatory Statement of the Committee of Conference.

[61]*Report of the Commission on Postal Service,* vol. 1 (April 18, 1977), p. 78.

[62]Ibid., p. 75.

[63]*Towards Postal Excellence,* June 1968, p. 4.

[64]Committee on Post Office and Civil Service, *Hearings on Postal Oversight,* 93rd Congress, 1st session, part 1, p. 11.

[65]*Congressional Record,* vol. 121 (September 29, 1975), pp. H9254-H9255.

[66]Ibid., p. H9256.

[67]Ibid.

[68]*Congressional Record,* vol. 121 (September 29, 1975), p. H9225, statement of Congressman David N. Henderson, chairman of the House Post Office and Civil Service Committee. Hard pressed as it has become, the Postal Service has, not surprisingly, made cuts. Many air taxi routes have been abandoned. Same-day delivery in downtown areas has been abandoned. Local mail has been mixed with area mail, slowing it down. Collections from corner mail deposit boxes have been restricted. The frequency of delivery in downtown business areas of our larger

cities has been cut. Door-to-door service in newly built-up areas is a thing of the past. And the criteria by which the fate of small rural offices is decided has been changed to facilitate a significant reduction in the number of such offices. Senate Report 94-966, pp. 3-4.

[69]Ibid., p. 8.

[70]*Congressional Record,* vol. 142 (August 27, 1976), p. S14305.

[71]Senate Report 94-966, letter from general counsel Louis Cox of the Postal Service dated March 18, 1976, to Senator Gale McGee, chairman of the Senate Committee on Post Office and Civil Service.

[72]House Report 94-391, letter from general counsel Louis Cox of the Postal Service dated July 18, 1975, to Congressman David Henderson, chairman of the House Post Office and Civil Service Committee.

[73]Ibid.

[74]*Congressional Record,* vol. 121 (September 29, 1975), p. H9223.

[75]Ibid., vol. 121 (October 30, 1975), p. H10444.

[76]Some claim that subsidies have the best incentive effect when they are awarded per unit of service. See, for example, the comments on this point in Elizabeth E. Bailey, "Peak-Load Pricing under Regulatory Constraint," *Journal of Political Economy,* vol. 80 (July-August 1972), pp. 662-79.

[77]*Report of the Commission on Postal Service,* April 18, 1977, vol. 1, p. 6.

[78]*Congressional Record,* vol. 121 (September 29, 1975), p. H9225.

[79]See Senate Report 94-966, p. 4.

[80]House Report 94-391, letter from Louis A. Cox, general counsel of the Postal Service to Congressman David N. Henderson, chairman of the House Committee on Post Office and Civil Service, dated July 18, 1975.

[81]"Few Postal Changes Sought," The *Washington Post,* September 21, 1977, p. E1.

[82]Ibid.

[83]Ibid.

[84]*Towards Postal Excellence,* June 1968, p. 4.

[85]The system of numbering sections in the bill is slightly different from those under current law. For consistency with references to this section made elsewhere in the bill, the numbering will have to be altered from that currently in the bill.

[86]"Few Postal Changes Sought," September 21, 1977, p. E1.

[87]Ibid.

[88] *Report of the Commission on Postal Service,* April 18, 1977, vol. 1, pp. 85-86.

[89] Ibid., p. 93.

[90] See *U.S. Postal Service: Reorganization Proposals* (Washington, D.C.: American Enterprise Institute, July 1976), pp. 21-25.

[91] 39 U.S.C. 3622(b)(3).

[92] 39 U.S.C. 403(c).

[93] "Few Postal Changes Sought," September 21, 1977, p. E1.